STANDARD CHRISTMAS
PROGRAM BOOK

Compiled by
Pat Fittro

Cincinnati, Ohio

Permission is granted to reproduce this material for ministry purposes only—not for resale.

Scripture quotations marked (NIV) are taken from the HOLY BIBLE, NEW INTERNATIONAL VERSION®. NIV®. Copyright© 1973, 1978, 1984 by International Bible Society. Used by permission of Zondervan Publishing House. All rights reserved.

Standard Publishing, Cincinnati, Ohio
A division of Standex International Corporation
© 2001 by Standard Publishing

All rights reserved
Printed in the United States of America

ISBN 0-7847-1244-1

Contents

Recitations

    Easy 4

    Medium 7

    Difficult 11

Exercises 21

Programs

    As Prophets Foretold 25

    Time to Move 27

    What About Tomorrow? 30

    Christmas Happiness 33

    The Truth About Christmas 36

Thanksgiving 39

Easy

Welcome
Iris Gray Dowling

We welcome you to our program
  On this happy Christmas Day.
We want you to hear the
    message we bring,
  And the joyful words we say.

Welcome, Jesus
Cora M. Owen

Welcome, baby Jesus,
  On this very special day.
We are glad You're with us,
  As we celebrate today.

A Christmas Wish
Iris Gray Dowling

I can't say a big long piece
Since I'm just a wee little girl;
But there's one thing I know
    how to do,
And that's wish a Merry
    Christmas to you. *(Indicate audience.)*

Time of Happiness
Cora M. Owen

Christmas is a happy time.
  What a joyous season!
And it is a time of peace.
  Jesus is the reason.

Throughout the Year
Dolores Steger

May Christ, and all the
    Christmas cheer,
Remain with you throughout
    the year.

The First Christmas
Alyce Pickett

Jesus left Heaven long ago.
  He came to earth to be
A caring Friend and Savior,
  And I know He loves me.

The Gift That Counts
Dolores Steger

At Christmastime, boy, I get
    gifts
  In fabulous amounts.
But Jesus is the gift, I'll say,
  That really, truly counts.

Time to Give
Cora M. Owen

It's time to give.
  It's time to sing.
It's time to worship
  Christ the King.

Happy Day
Lillian Robbins

One, two, three, four,
I wish I could count some more.
But I know it's true,
Jesus came for you.
I hope you have a happy
    Christmas Day.

Another Birthday Candle
Dolores Steger

Another birthday candle,
  Dear Lord, I light for You,
And celebrate Your coming,
  Today and all year through.

The Best Gift
Helen C. Shambaugh

Mommy says don't worry
  If my gifts are very small.
She says if I wrap them up with
    love,
  They'll be the best gifts of all.

Bells Ringing for Jesus
Helen C. Shambaugh

I love to hear the church bells
    ring,
They tell me, *(child's name)* come
    and sing,
Come to worship, praise and
    pray,
Christ the Lord is born this day.

In Manger Bed
Dolores Steger

As to Christmas Day we head
And we see a brilliant spread
Of Christmas green and
    Christmas red
And gifts galore, let's think
    instead
Of Jesus, Lord, in manger bed.

Bigger Gift
Mary Ann Green

Faith is a gift
  That many times seems too
    small.
But as it grows
  It's the biggest gift of all.

The Shopping List
Dolores Steger

Your Christmas shopping list is
    long.
Take my advice, you won't go
    wrong.
Tear up your list, give everyone
The gift of love that's God's own
    Son.

Gift That Will Last
Mary Ann Green

I'd like to give a gift that will
    last.
I know, I'll give a Bible that will
Bless even after Christmas is
    past.

To Honor Him
Dolores Steger

To honor Him, the shepherds came,
  The wise men, they came too.
And who else came to honor Him?
  Did you? Did you? Will you?

The Birthday of Jesus
Dolores Steger

The time is so jolly,
With lights, bells and holly,
And gifts wrapped in red and in green,
But always remember
What comes in December:
The birthday of Jesus, I mean.

Thanks for Coming
Iris Gray Dowling

Thanks for coming here today
  To worship Christ, the newborn King;
We hope you leave with hearts of joy
  And songs you'll always want to sing.

Christmas
Alta McLain

A Baby born in Bethlehem
  Was much like you and me.
He was born that we might live.
  The Son of God is He.

Angel
Mary Ann Green

The angel told the shepherds
  Of the Baby born that day.
They said, "Go. You will find Him
  There, fast asleep on the hay."

Who's the Baby?
Iris Gray Dowling

A Babe was born in Bethlehem,
  Does any person know His name?
How sad when no one seems to care
  God's Son was the one who came!

Happy Birthday
Dolores Steger

Happy Birthday, little One;
Happy Birthday, God's sweet Son;
Happy Birthday; may You be
Always close and dear to me.

Summon the Angels
Dolores Steger

Summon the angels with trumpets and harps,
  Summon them so they may sing
Anthems of joy, for to us now is born
  A Savior named Jesus, the King.

Medium

Christmas Welcome
Lillian Robbins

We welcome you,
    That's really true,
    To the program we have
    planned.

Just a simple way
    That we can say
    Jesus came to save man.
        This is our Christmas
    presentation for you.

Lights
Dolores Steger

Lights in the windows are all
    aglow,
Shining to let all mankind know
It's Christmas!

Lights in the heavens, stars
    burning bright,
Telling the world this is the
    night,
It's Christmas!

Lights in the stable warming the
    scene
Where a Babe lies; what do they
    mean?
It's Christmas!

The Reasons Why
Cora M. Owen

Do you know the reason why
    We celebrate today?
It's because the King of kings
    Was born on Christmas Day.

Do you know the reason why
    Our hearts are full of joy?
It's because God sent to earth,
    His precious Baby Boy.

Celebrate the Birthday
Dolores Steger

We celebrate the birthday,
    The birthday of a King;
Be joyous; give all praise to God;
    Sound trumpets, anthems sing.

We celebrate the birthday;
    Raise voices in accord,
With hymns of love, devotion for
    The birthday of our Lord.

Shining Light
Cora M. Owen

Each time I see a Christmas light,
All glistening and shining bright
I think of how Christ came to be
Light of the world, that all may
    see.

Each time I see a twinkling star,
Shining on earth from skies afar,
I think of how Christ came one
    night,
To be an everlasting light.

Happy Birthday, Jesus
Dolores Steger

Happy birthday, Jesus;
  It's wonderful to see
The celebration of the day
  You came to set man free.

Happy birthday, Jesus;
  I'm thankful as can be
That to Your birthday party
    now,
  You have invited me.

It's Sweet
Cora M. Owen

It's sweet to think of Christmas
    past
  That happened long ago.
It's sweet to have the memories,
  That stay with such a glow.

It's sweet to make new
    memories,
  With family and friends.
We'll have them all to think
    about,
  So they will never end.

Another Lovely Christmas Scene
Nell Ford Hann

What is white?
    What is green?
Another lovely
    Christmas scene.
Of holly leaves,
    Mistletoe;
Angel wings
    And lacy snow.
What is red?
    What is green?
Another lovely
    Christmas scene.
Of poinsettias,
    Candles bright;
'Tis Jesus' birthday,
    This holy night.

Arctic Snowmen
Nell Ford Hann

I always like to think of Arctic
    snowmen,
  Arriving around this special
    time of year;
When folks are making plans
    with friends and family,
  As another Christmas Day is
    drawing near.
When the heat's on, the snow-
    men leave so quickly,
  They only stick around in
    chilling weather;
Jesus comes with healing in His
    hands,
  And a promise that He will
    leave you never.

Sweet Notes
Cora M. Owen

Oh, what sweet notes of music,
   The angel chorus sang.
That night throughout the
   heavens
   Their joyous message rang.

Oh, what sweet notes were
   rendered,
   By voices that were sweet.
To tell the news of Jesus.
   Let us their songs repeat.

Christmases Past
Nell Ford Hann

As we reflect upon Christmases
   past,
And think back on that first
   birthday;
We ponder on precious images,
Of baby Jesus . . . asleep on the
   hay.
As we make plans for the
   birthday party,
That has become a season, you
   know;
Christmas did not bring us
   Christ,
Christ gave us Christmas . . .
   long, long ago.

A Long Time
Cora M. Owen

It was two thousand years ago,
   When Jesus came from Heaven.
Because He loved all humans so,
   This precious gift was given.

It has been such a long, long
   time,
   Yet Jesus Christ is real.
He lives within my heart today.
   His presence I can feel.

Miracle of Christmas
Cora M. Owen

The miracle of Christmas,
   When God became a man,
And came to bring salvation
   According to God's plan.

The miracle of Christmas,
   When God himself came down
On a lovely starlit night
   Into Bethlehem town.

The Bells
Dolores Steger

Hear the bells ringing
   For joy and for mirth;
Hear the bells ringing
   For a blessing's worth;
Hear the bells ringing
   For peace upon earth;
Hear the bells ringing
   For Lord Jesus' birth.

Little Babe
Dolores Steger

Little Babe, little Babe,
  There in the stall,
Sleeping so peacefully,
  You look so small;
Soon You will grow
  To be taller than tall;
You'll be a Savior
  To rule over all.

Hey There, Little Baby
Dolores Steger

Hey there, little Baby,
  Born so long ago,
Christmastime is here now,
  And I truly know
That You're always with me,
  From me You'll not go;
Hey there, Baby Jesus,
  Oh, I love You so.

What Does Christmas Mean to Me?
Dolores Steger

What does Christmas mean to
  me?
  Please pardon while I pause;
Does it mean presents that I get?
  Does it mean Santa Claus?

No, that's not so; it really means
  The birth of Christ, you see;
He's in my heart to stay and
   that's
  What Christmas means to me.

God's Way
Helen Kitchell Evans

This morning I vow to face
  All situations of my life;
I vow to overcome those things
  That fill my days with strife.

This morning I will stand fast
  I'll use my faith much more;
I'll look for brighter outcomes
  Knowing there is good in store.

I'll have the faith of Mary,
  The faith on that special night,
For with God there is a way
  And everything will turn out
   right.

Joyful!
Cora M. Owen

Christmas! What a joyful time!
  With many things aglow.
And we hear the chimes sing
   out
  Music of long ago.

Christmas! What a joyful sound!
  When bells ring loud and clear.
Heralding a season sweet
  With songs we love to hear.

Christmas! What a joyful word!
  We listen to the tale
That's when Jesus Christ was
   born,
  And men and angels hail.

Difficult

Most Precious Christmas Gift
Kay Hoffman

Shopping for Christmas gifts I
   pondered
  That night of long ago
When the magi brought their
   priceless gifts
  To the Babe in manger low.

And yet, their gifts of royal
   wealth
  Did pale that holy night
As they gazed upon the Christ
   child,
  God's gift of love and light.

God sent His Christmas gift for
   all,
  One of eternal worth;
The most precious gift He had
   to give
  The blessed Savior's birth.

Wrapping Love
Helen C. Shambaugh

Shining paper of foil so bright,
  Red, blue, gold, silver and
    green,
Tissue paper of white and other
   hues,
  Wrapping paper with a
    Christmas scene.

In these we wrap gifts for our
   family,
  Our friends and the neighbors
    we know,
We want our gifts to be beautiful
  Our love for them to show.

We choose the gifts so carefully,
  Hoping they'll be just right
To bring sweet joy to the heart
   of each one,
  Oh, what a beautiful sight!

But the Gift Mary wrapped in
   swaddling clothes
  None better could ever be,
For God gave this Gift, His
   beloved Son,
  Our Savior forever to be!

It Happened
Cora M. Owen

It happened. Oh, so long ago
When Jesus came to dwell below.
There was a bright and shining
   star,
Seen by wise men from afar.

There was a lovely angel song,
Shepherds heard the notes so
   strong,
And listened to a message clear:
"Christ is born in a manger
   near."

It happened. They so quickly went
To see the Savior—Heaven-sent.
He was found on a bed of hay.
What rejoicing on that day!

All the Promises God Has Made
Nell Ford Hann

All the promises God has made,
  Are sealed in the blood of
    Jesus;
We are heirs of all things in
    Christ,
  For that is the way God sees
    us.

He sees us all as winners,
  When we know Him that is
    our style,
Though we walk in God's favor,
  He has no favorite child.

All the promises God has made,
  He fulfilled on that Bethlehem
    night;
When He sent His Son to the
    world,
  Wise men yet seek the Light!

All the promises God has made,
  Are awesome to behold . . . and
    ponder;
For He loved us so much . . . He
    gave . . .
  O, God of love . . . O, God of
    wonder!

That Night in Bethlehem
Kay Hoffman

He came in the darkness of
    night,
  The little promised King
Only a few would see His star
  Or hear the angels sing.

Wrapped in swaddling cloths
    He lay
  In a humble stable stall.
The little Babe from Heaven sent
  The Savior born for all.

Magi, star-led, brought royal
    gifts
  Myrrh, frankincense and gold.
Poor shepherds gave all they
    had,
  A wee lamb from their fold.

The cattle knelt in reverence
  Although they knew not why
While shepherds and the magi
    prayed
  On bended knee nearby.

The mother gazed upon her
    Babe
  And pondered in her heart
How God would choose a poor
    young maid
  To play this special part.

The angels sang sweet lullabies
  Till came the morning light
When Christ was born in
    Bethlehem,
  A truly awesome night!

The Shepherds' Example
Sonja Turner

I like to think of Christmas
  When the shepherds saw a
    light
And heard the angels singing
  Under starry skies so bright.

The shepherds heard the good
    news
  That in Bethlehem they'd see,
The Messiah that was born
  And would set the people free.

So they left their flocks and
    went
  To the stable rough and spare,
And saw the newborn Baby
  Lying in a manger there.

They bowed their heads and
    worshiped
  With a plain and humble way,
And knelt before the Savior,
  In His cradle made of hay.

We, too, can worship Jesus
  As the shepherds did of old,
If we open up our hearts
  To the greatest story told.

Signs of the Times
Sonja Turner

December points to Christmas.
  It's time to wait and see
What surprises are in store
  For my family and me.

In malls and shops and down-
    town
  Wreaths and holly soon appear.
Jingle bells and colored lights
  Tell us Christmastime is near.

The radio plays carols,
  Those old songs we love to
    sing.
The air is filled with music,
  And we hear the church bells
    ring.

We plan to visit old friends,
  And all our relatives, too,
Taking some gifts and cookies
  And sharing our joy anew.

With Santa Claus and presents
  And a decorated tree,
We're ready for the season
  As excited as can be.

All these things are wonderful
  But the very best by far,
Is the birth of one Baby
  Under a Bethlehem star.

That Baby was Christ Jesus
  Who came in a humble way,
And lay on a manger bed
  That very first Christmas Day.

Turned Away
Cora M. Owen

The crowds in Bethlehem that
    night—
  They did not know or care
That Jesus Christ, God's only
    Son,
  Would make appearance there.

The people in that city then
  Did not know what they
    missed;
Because the Christ was turned
    away,
  Much blessing they dismissed.

The precious Savior of the world
  He still is turned away
By those who do not realize
  Just who He is today.

The Angel's Call
Dolores Steger

Oh, shepherds on the hillsides,
  Leave the dark of night,
Go to Bethlehem and see
  A Child of hope and light.

Oh, shepherds on the hillsides,
  Greet the Babe who came
To save the world and mankind,
  Immanuel's His name.

Oh, shepherds on the hillsides,
  So that all may learn
Of the Savior, spread the news,
  When to flocks you return.

Wise Men Indeed
Joseph C. Mullins

They were certainly wise,
  For they followed the star;
They followed its bidding
  Though it led them far.

They were certainly wise,
  They brought gold, of all
    things;
Nothing more fitting
  For the King of kings.

They were certainly wise,
  For myrrh they gave
To prepare for His burial
  In the impotent grave.

They were certainly wise,
  For frankincense so fine
They gave to the Child,
  The infant divine.

Appropriate gifts did
  The wise men bring
As kneeling they worshiped
  The newborn King.

Let us also be wise
  In this time of giving;
And give to Him
  Who's our reason for living.

The gift of service,
  The gift of love,
And let us worship
  The Child from above.

The Boy Who Saw the Star
Margaret Primrose

I gasped as I saw a big bright star
That moved across the sky.
Then it stopped and stood over a little house.
But how could this be and why?

Some kings were lumbering toward our little town
On the backs of camels that swayed.
The men's eyes were fixed on the traveling star
That had led them to where it stayed.

When they knelt by the side of a Baby's bed
To offer Him spices and gold,
It was something that only wise men do
With all their hands may hold.

In the depths of the night God spoke in a dream
And commanded the kings to flee,
For Herod would vainly try to kill
The Child they came to see.

When I woke near dawn, I heard them leave
By a different road than they came,
And because I know the story is true,
I will never be the same.

The Colors Red and Green
Nell Ford Hann

The crimson cardinal flits about,
    Then perches on the bough of a pine;
As I look upon this feathered beauty,
    A vision swiftly comes to mind.

All through the year they are around,
    The bright red bird and the lush green tree;
Why . . . they are dressed in Christmas colors,
    For all the world to see.

The well-formed rose that blooms in season
    From its coddled, noble bed;
To the luscious, plump strawberries,
    That have ripened to fire-engine red.

From our abundant summer garden,
    With folks and kin we share red tomatoes;
I was talking with some neighbors,
    Who are growing red potatoes.

When I look around I can see,
    Red and green . . . prevalent the entire year;
Jesus is present, not just at Christmas,
    But every day . . . ever near.

Boundless Love
Lillian Robbins

Such love is a boundless energy
  That springs up in the heart of
    man.
It isn't something we can touch
  Or really can understand.

But God's wonderful love for all
  of us
  Was revealed in a special way.
He gave the best in all the world
  On that blessed Christmas Day.

People didn't call it Christmas
  then,
  The day of Jesus' birth;
But regardless of the word we
  speak,
  It's joy around the earth.

The people knew a Messiah
  would come.
  They didn't know where or
    when,
But God was planning His own
  way
  To forgive mankind of sin.

His dear Son to a virgin was born.
  To Mary the chosen maid.
And in that time in the stillness
  of night,
  In a manger Jesus was laid.

What love could allow the most
  glorious Gem
  Even God could hold so dear
To leave the home in Heaven
  with Him
  To come and still man's fear.

We look before at Joseph's plight
  As he arrived in Bethlehem
    town.
Could find no place for Mary to
  be
  But on straw laid on the
    ground.

There was abundant love
  around that night
  Though the citizens didn't
    share.
For Mary who needed a bed to
  rest,
  They didn't even seem to care.

But God looked down and kept
  them safe,
  The woman He'd chosen and
    the Babe,
And Joseph, in his role as
  planned
  When Jesus came forth to save.

God's love poured out more
  than we know
  In that place on that holy night
To provide for us salvation from
  sin;
  God's plan when the time was
    right.

No wonder Christmas means
  such amazing joy.
  It began to honor Jesus' birth.
Such amazing love and amazing
  grace
  To all the folks on earth.

Be happy and thrilled this Christmastime
  As you accept the gift God gave.
Never forget it's in God's own Son,
  He said that we could be saved.

When Jesus Christ Was Born
Cora M. Owen

As shepherds watched their flock of sheep
And Bethlehem was fast asleep,
The stars shone down on a night so deep.
  When Jesus Christ was born.

Then angel choir did appear,
Singing a joyous song of cheer.
They announced, "A Savior is here."
  When Jesus Christ was born.

The shepherds found Him in the hay.
They worshiped Jesus where He lay.
The Son of God on earth that day.
  When Jesus Christ was born.

There's Nothing Like Christmas
Dolores Steger

There's nothing like Christmas
   that comes to my mind;
It's special, a day that is one of a kind;
That's why I am here and I've come to remind
Everyone now that I hope you will find
The promise that came with the Baby, who lay
So silently sleeping that glorious day,
And open your heart to Him; there let Him stay,
An image of joy that will ne'er fade away.

A Symbol of Christmas
Dolores Steger

A symbol of Christmas,
  What would it be?
A wreath or a candle,
  A bright, lighted tree,
A stocking, a Santa,
  A bell, ring-a-ling,
A sleigh or a reindeer,
  A popped popcorn string,
An angel, a halo,
  A crown or a star,
A manger, a shepherd,
  A wise man from far?
A symbol of Christmas
  God's Son from above?
It should be a heart;
  He's the symbol of love.

Rejoicing Ones
Cora M. Owen

The angels rejoiced when Christ came down.
  They showed it as they praised.
Their words announced Him to the earth,
  And joyous songs they raised.
The shepherds rejoiced when He was born.
  They hurried to His side.
They found the Babe in manger bed,
  And God they glorified.
The wise men rejoiced when Jesus came.
  They found the holy Child.
Presented there the choicest gifts.
  I'm sure that Jesus smiled.
His mother rejoiced within her heart,
  When she saw the infant One.
She knew He was a special child
  For He was God's own Son.

Jesus Is at the Heart
Tobi Anne Tate

Jesus is at the heart of this season
  Which is good, I suppose, in a way;
But to me it only stands to reason,
  He should be at the heart of each day.
Caroling, shopping . . . church attendance is strong,
  After all, it is Christmas, you see.
Jesus must be the heart of each day all year long,
  Not just thought of while trimming the tree.
The shopping and wrapping . . . and even gift-giving,
  The singing of songs of His birth;
Mean nothing unless He's our reason for living,
  Then there will be real peace on earth!

I See
Dolores Steger

There it stands, the Christmas tree,
Decorated beautifully; tell me what on it you see.
I see the lights that are twinkling so bright;
They look like the stars on that first Christmas night.
I see the tinsel on boughs, their array
Reminds me of straw on which baby Jesus lay.
I see the garlands wind through branches green,
Like pathways of shepherds to the manger scene.
I see the balls, precious, rare they appear,
And think of the gifts wise men brought the Child dear.
I see the angel set high up above,
And know that in Jesus, God sent to us love.
There it stands, the Christmas tree,
Decorated beautifully.
May you,
Through it,
Jesus see.

Happiness at Christmas
Lillian Robbins

I wish you **peace**—a still, quiet place in your heart where you feel assurance that every obstacle can become a stepping-stone and every victory can be a propeller to lift you to new heights.
I wish you **joy**—the ecstasy that lightens up your life with the exuberance of a mighty waterfall that cascades down a mountainside.
I wish you **contentment**—the attitude that allows you to control desires that may otherwise force you into a constant battle of seeking that which is beyond your reach.
I wish you **love**—that all-consuming emotion that binds you to those near and dear, but loosens its cords enough to allow you to reach out to others.
And finally, I wish you **happiness**—a life that combines **peace, joy, contentment,** and **love** in fullest measure.
All of these wishes can come true through the Christ child whose birth we celebrate. Have a blessed Christmas.

Christmas All Year Long
Dixie Phillips

I tuck a little Christmas inside my little heart,
When I sing a Christmas carol and memorize my part.

I hide it in my heart, because I love it so,
It warms my cold heart through the January snow.

When the winds begin to blow on a February day,
I keep a little Christmas as I bow my head to pray.

In March and April, as the rains begin to fall,
Christmas floods my heart when on God's name I call.

In the month of May, as the tulips start to bloom,
Christmas joy fills my heart and I hum a happy tune!

In June and July, just to beat the summer heat,
I read the Christmas story, so precious to repeat.

In the month of August, when school bus appears,
The Christmas story chases away all my fears.

In September and October when the leaves fall from the tree,
You will find me so thankful that He was born for me.

Then there is November and Thanksgiving Day,
Our teacher gets us ready for the Christmas play.

Finally, December comes . . . it is so exciting.
All our relatives to our Christmas play we're inviting.

Now you know why I celebrate Christmas all year long
And why there's nothing better than a Christmas song.

Exercises

Four Gifts
Dolores Steger

CHILD 1:
Here's a gift of gold I bring,
For the newborn baby King;

CHILD 2:
Here's some myrrh so soothing, mild,
As is this most holy Child;

CHILD 3:
I present Him incense sweet,

ALL:
But our gifts are not complete;
So on bended knee we bow,
And give love to the Babe right now.

Finding the Best
Margaret Primrose

FIRST CHILD:
They napped day by day on the desert sand
While they followed a star to a distant land.
Thirsty and hungry and longing for home—
We call them wise men. Why did they roam?

SECOND CHILD:
They were taking gifts to the King of kings,
And found the joy that knowing Him brings.
So why not kneel and be truly blest
By offering to Jesus our very best?

Wise Men
Dolores Steger

CHILD 1:
Wise men, wise men,
Where do you go
Journeying o'er mountains high
And through valleys low?
Wise men, wise men,
Where do you go?
Truly, truly tell me;
I really want to know.

THREE CHILDREN:
We go, we go,
As ancient prophets said,
Traveling through unknown lands
By a bright star led.
We go, we go,
To a manger bed,
Where a Babe, a King of kings,
Rests there His tiny head.

We Know About God's Love
Iris Gray Dowling

CHILD 1 *(turning to Child 2 & 3):*
We know God sent His Son to earth,
His love was the reason why.

CHILD 2:
We know that Christ was born in Bethlehem,
And on the cross He would have to die.

CHILD 3:
We know He rose to life again,
And He'll take us to Heaven by and by.

ALL THREE CHILDREN:
We hope you know and accept God's love today.

(Use motions for the underlined words as follows:
know—point fingers to forehead
love—cross arms over chest
cross—make cross with fingers
rose—bring hands upward
Heaven—point up to sky
you—point toward audience)

At the Manger
Alyce Pickett

CHILD 1:
I wish I could have gone that night
To the stable where He lay—
The little Baby Jesus sweet
In a manger filled with hay.

CHILD 2:
I would have kissed His little cheek,
Then I would try to sing
A lullaby like my mom does—
To please the little King.

CHILD 3:
I'm glad that Jesus came to earth.
I know He came to be
A Savior-Friend for everyone,
And He loves you and me.

Tell the Good News!
Alyce Pickett

CHILD 1:
Come with me, let's go
Tell all the people so
All the world will know
About Jesus.

CHILD 2:
Tell them how He lay
On manger bed hay
That first Christmas Day.
Baby Jesus.

CHILD 3:
Tell everyone that He
Came to earth to be
Savior for you and me . . .
Lord Jesus.

ALL:
Today He is the same
Loving Lord who came.
Let us praise His name!
Our Jesus.

Optional: Sing carol of choice with offstage choir.

Why We Celebrate
Helen C. Shambaugh

CHILD 1: *(Holds small nativity scene.)*
Why do Christians celebrate
This season every year?
Because Jesus was born in Bethlehem
This fills our hearts with cheer.

CHILD 2: *(Holds Bible.)*
We read it in the Bible
The story is in Luke two,
How God once sent His Son to earth,
To be our salvation true.

CHILD 3: *(Holds a small cross.)*
So we must ever remember
Amid gifts and tinsel so bright,
Jesus came to die on a cross,
To make all wrong things right.

CHILD 4: *(Holds a battery-operated lighted candle.)*
Jesus has risen again to glory,
Forever our Light to be.
If we obey, He will someday take us
To live in His light eternally.

CHILD 5: *(Holds wand in hand; [could be dowel or stick with star glued to end] touches article in each child's hand with wand as it is named.)*
Nativity, Bible, Cross and Light,
Yes! We celebrate this season
With love in our hearts for God above,
King Jesus is the reason!

The Light of the World
Carolyn R. Scheidies

For six individuals or groups

MEDLEY: *(first stanzas of "Joy to the World," "Angels, from the Realms of Glory," "Hark! the Herald Angels Sing")*

NARRATOR: Luke 2:1-7

SONG: "O Little Town of Bethlehem" *(first stanza)*

1: *(hold up large star)*
The Light of the World was not the star,
Which shown over Bethlehem long ago.
The Light of the World was a special baby,
Born in the stable below.

2: *(hold up manger scene)*
He was not just any baby,
Born in the usual way,
But the Son of God from a virgin birth,
In a manger filled with hay.

3. *(hold up picture of angels with the shepherds)*
He was the Messiah, the Savior
As prophesied from of old,
As witnessed by the angels,
And the shepherds they had told.

NARRATOR: Luke 2:8-17

SONG: "O Little Town of Bethlehem" *(second stanza)*

4. *(hold up large Bible)*
Like you and me He suffered,
That He might understand,
For He came not just as a baby,
But as part of the Master's plan.

5. *(hold up cross or picture of Jesus on the cross)*
He came to us, this Jesus,
To live as we, but more;
He died upon the cross and rose,
To open Heaven's door.

NARRATOR: Isaiah 9:6

SONG: "O Little Town of Bethlehem" *(third stanza)*

6: *(picture of Jesus)*
The light of the world is Jesus,
Savior-Lord to you and me,
He only asks we let Him in,
That He might set us free.

SONG: "O Little Town of Bethlehem" *(last stanza)*

ALL: Matthew 5:16

As Prophets Foretold
Carolyn R. Scheidies

Characters:
NARRATOR
CHORUS, consisting of three groups of voices: High, Low, and Medium
MARY and JOSEPH in appropriate costume
SHEPHERDS in costume

Props: Stable scene with cross overhead, doll

Scriptures are from the *New International Version* of the Bible.

NARRATOR: "For to us a child is born, to us a son is given, and the government will be on his shoulders. And he will be called Wonderful Counselor, Mighty God, Everlasting Father, Prince of Peace. Of the increase of his government and peace there will be no end. He will reign on David's throne and over his kingdom, establishing and upholding it with justice and righteousness from that time on and forever" (Isaiah 9: 6, 7).

LOW VOICES: Jesus came as the prophets foretold,
MEDIUM VOICES: God's own dear Son,
LOW VOICES: Came not as a conquering hero,
HIGH VOICES: But as a baby . . . God's holy One.

(Mary, sitting center stage, cradles child. Joseph stands beside her.)

NARRATOR: "'She will give birth to a son, and you are to give him the name Jesus, because he will save his people from their sins.' All this took place to fulfill what the Lord had said through the prophet: 'The virgin will be with child and will give birth to a son, and they will call him Immanuel,' which means, 'God with us'" (Matthew 1:21-23).

HIGH VOICES: For the Baby born in Bethlehem's stable
LOW VOICES: Died at Calvary,
   And conquered death and Hell that He
MEDIUM VOICES: Might set His people free.

NARRATOR: "The people walking in darkness have seen a great light; on those living in the land of the shadow of death a light has dawned" (Isaiah 9:2).
SHEPHERDS: "Come, Thou Long-Expected Jesus" *(center stage, half-turned toward cross and manger, sing first stanza)*
LOW VOICES: *(join in for second stanza)*
ALL: For Jesus came to bring us hope,
MEDIUM VOICES: Came to save us from our sin,
Came that we might be made whole,
LOW VOICES: As we ask Him to live within.

(Shepherds kneel in worship.)

NARRATOR: "The Spirit of the Lord is on me, because he has anointed me to preach good news to the poor. He has sent me to proclaim freedom for the prisoners and recovery of sight for the blind, to release the oppressed, to proclaim the year of the Lord's favor" (Luke 4:18, 19).
MEDIUM VOICES: "Blessed Be the Name" *(sing first stanza)*
LOW VOICES: *(join in on refrain only)*
HIGH VOICES: *(sing third stanza)*
ALL: *(sing refrain)*
HIGH VOICES: As we celebrate this Christmas,
MEDIUM VOICES: Let us bow before the One, *(all kneel)*
LOW VOICES: Who brought us hope, as the prophets foretold,
ALL: Jesus Christ . . . God's Son.
NARRATOR: "Come to me, all you who are weary and burdened, and I will give you rest" (Matthew 11:28).
ALL: "Joy to the World!" *(rise and sing stanzas one and two)*

Time to Move
Margaret Primrose

Characters:
TYLER, KAYLA AND BOBBY—brothers and sister
HALEY AND JON—friends who come to visit
LADY—to sing "Count Your Blessings" (offstage)

Setting and Props: A family room with moving boxes and things that need to be packed.

BOBBY *(entering the room with boxes and things to pack):* Come on in this room, Haley and Jon. I'm afraid we won't have time for fun and games today, but at least we can talk to you.
JON: Hey! What's going on?
TYLER: We have to help Mom pack.
HALEY: Well, we knew you were going to move, but we didn't expect to find you packing this soon.
KAYLA: It was a surprise to us, too. As you know, Dad's already gone south to his new job and Mom's been trying to sell the house so our family can be together again. All of a sudden, a man wanted to buy our house. His house burned so he wants to have his family in this one by Christmas.
JON: By Christmas? That's only three days away. Where will you spend Christmas?
TYLER: Who knows? Maybe in a moving truck or the car.
HALEY: I thought you'd at least be here for the Sunday school program and to go caroling. Mrs. Green always has big batches of homemade cookies and hot chocolate when we sing for her.
BOBBY: Sorry! We're going to have to miss it all.
HALEY: Couldn't you ask the new owner for just a few more days?
KAYLA: Mom and Dad don't think we should. The buyer and his wife have five children and are badly in need of a house.
HALEY: What about you? You need a house too.
KAYLA: Dad found one for us. He's spending all the time he can to make sure it's ready for us. I wasn't any happier than Tyler and Bobby were about this move. Then I started thinking about Mary and Joseph and their long trip to Bethlehem to pay taxes. At least we don't have to walk or ride a donkey for days to get where we're going.

TYLER: But we won't get to go to Grandma's house for Christmas dinner.
KAYLA: We're going there tonight for an early Christmas dinner. That's good, isn't it?
BOBBY: Sure. We'll at least get to open some of our Christmas presents early.
TYLER: But how are we going to find room to play with them in the car?
JON: That's a good question.
KAYLA: There are games we can play without toys, and Mom told us we get to take turns riding with Uncle Bob in the truck.
BOBBY: Well, he is a good storyteller.
JON: If he's as good as my dad at that, I'd trade the toys for stories any day.
HALEY: Hmm. When the kids had to go to Bethlehem with their parents to pay taxes, don't you suppose they got plenty tired of walking? You can be pretty sure they didn't play with video games and roller blades along the way. Maybe their dads were good storytellers.
BOBBY: Yeah, but I hope we'll find good motels the two nights of the trip.
HALEY: That might be hard, because lots of people travel at Christmastime.
JON: I've heard that lots of restaurants are closed too. Where will you eat?
KAYLA: At fast-food places, Mom says some of them will stay open.
BOBBY: She said that? Hey, if we get to eat hamburgers and French fries on Christmas Day, it will be the first time. They're my favorites, not turkey and dressing.
HALEY: Ours too.
JON: Well, what do you know? I've started to wish I could go with you.
TYLER: We might have to camp a night or two in our new house because it will take time to unload the truck.
JON: I love to camp.
KAYLA: Mom says she's putting the sleeping bags in the trunk of the car where they'll be easy to find.
HALEY: Unlike Mary and Joseph, you won't have to sniff all those barnyard smells.
KAYLA: Am I glad for that!
BOBBY: You know, of all the Christmases we've ever had this one will probably be the most like the first Christmas. That's not all bad.
HALEY: And maybe you can call us to tell us all about it.
KAYLA: That's more than Mary and Joseph could have done.

(The children hear singing in the background.)

HALEY: Who's singing?
BOBBY: It's just Mom. She likes to sing that old song her grandma taught her when she was a little girl.

(Children listen to the chorus of "Count Your Blessings" and clap when she finishes.)

See How We Journey
Dolores Steger

ALL: See how we journey, we've come from afar,
We've faithfully followed a heavenly star;
We're going to honor the King of all kings,
And these are the treasurers that each of us brings:

WISE MAN 1: I bring Him incense; its fragrance so mild
Will waft 'round the crib of this sweet, gentle Child;

WISE MAN 2: I bring Him myrrh; may its lotion caress
The Babe as He lies in His pure blessedness;

WISE MAN 3: I bring Him gold, hoping this treasure shows
The love and the joy from which my heart now flows.

ALL: See how we journey and soon we'll come near,
Near to the place where the Baby so dear
Blissfully, peacefully, tenderly lies,
Under the heavens and star-studded skies.

What About Tomorrow?
Lillian Robbins

Characters:
NARRATOR
MOTHER (Cynthia)
KIT

Scene: Child's bedroom

NARRATOR: It had been a hard day for Cynthia. Work was piled up at the office. On the way from day care, Sammy hadn't wanted to ride in the car seat. And while Cynthia was preparing supper, she wasn't really in the mood for that continual conversation with Kit. Finally though, the baby was asleep. Cynthia would be able to relax after she got Kit to bed. But first there must be that extended good-night time. Kit never wanted to settle down.

(Kit and Cynthia enter. Kit goes to the bed and lies down, but immediately she sits up.)

KIT: Mom, what is the most important thing about tomorrow?
MOTHER *(sitting on the bed):* For one thing it is a new day. Now just close your eyes and go to sleep.
KIT: That's not enough. Tell me more.
MOTHER: It will be a day the Lord will make. And of course you know it is Christmas Eve.
KIT: Tell me about it again, Mom. Tell me about the Baby born in a stable.
MOTHER: Many years ago . . .
KIT: I know that part. Mary lived in Nazareth and Joseph was a carpenter. Mom, why didn't Jesus get born to a king?
MOTHER: Well, Kit, God has a good purpose for all His plans.
KIT: Sure, if Jesus was a king, He could never be a good friend to us. We couldn't talk to Him and ask Him for things either.
MOTHER: That's a thought. Now back to the story. You know Mary and Joseph had to go a long way to get to Bethlehem, and it was not easy to travel then as it is now. There were no fine cars to ride in. There were no paved streets and superhighways. Most of the time when

people traveled, they just walked. Or maybe sometimes, a person would ride on the back of a donkey.

KIT: God could have just put Mary and Joseph on a magic carpet and sent them to Bethlehem.

MOTHER: Yes, but Mary didn't get special treatment. And Jesus got no preference just because He was God's Son. He was like other babies, born to a young woman, grew up like other boys, and became a man who worked like other men. Of course He was different, too, because He was born of a virgin, and He was God's own Son. He knows us and loves us in a very special way; and we know Him and love Him in a special way.

KIT: I just wish He could have had a nice clean room to be born in.

MOTHER: He didn't really need a room, Kit. If He had, God would have made it possible even though the inn was full. Mary and Joseph had a very private place where they could really be alone. It was a perfect setting for the birth of Jesus. We may not think so, but God always knows best.

KIT: Go on, Mom tell me all about it. Why didn't someone help Mary and Joseph? They could see she was going to have a baby.

MOTHER: But of course they didn't know the baby was God's Son.

KIT: I wonder if they would have helped if they had known. The other day when the governor came to our school, everyone was busy getting the rooms in order and cleaning the halls and grounds. The principal told us to be on good behavior. And the governor is just a man. What if Jesus were coming?

MOTHER: That is a good question. Maybe people think more about that when it is Christmastime.

KIT: You know what I think is cool? That Jesus was just a little baby, like our little Sammy. People could touch His little hands, feel His soft skin, rock Him to sleep, and give Him a little kiss on the cheek. It is like—well, I guess like He was just one of us, but a lot better than any of us.

MOTHER: You're right, Kit. God's wisdom is so wonderful He planned for our Savior to come to us just that way. You remember we read that He would be called Immanuel, which means "God with us." So Jesus knows how it feels to be excited and thrilled or to be lonely and sad. He knows how happy we are when we get what we want and how disappointed we are when things just don't work out for us.

KIT: And He loves us just like you and Dad love Sammy and me.

MOTHER: That's right, Kit. I think one of the most important things about Jesus is how He loves everyone, not just the rich man on the hill or the star athletes or the kings of countries, but He loves Alonza and

Helen and Kasandra and Twilia and everyone, just as He loves you and me.

KIT: Mom, I'm glad Jesus was born on Christmas. It makes me feel all comfy and safe, kind of quiet inside like there is always somebody there who is my own special friend.

MOTHER: You're right, Honey. He is your special friend and He will be forever, even when you get older. *(Gives Kit a hug.)*

KIT: Mom, I bet Jesus' hugs are great—yours are.

MOTHER: Better than mine, Kit! His arms are the arms of God.

KIT: Can I just say a short prayer tonight, Mom?

MOTHER: If you want to.

KIT *(kneels beside bed):* Thank You, God, for Christmas and for baby Jesus. Amen. *(Gets back in bed and lies down.)*

MOTHER: Now just close your eyes and go to sleep. Good night, my precious one.

(Lights out and Cynthia leaves.)

NARRATOR: Cynthia walked into the hall. The hard day was past. There was joy in her heart. It was true that tomorrow was another day that the Lord would make, and the blessings she received were always innumerable. The Lord Jesus held her hand all the way. What a marvelous blessing of Christmas.

Christmas Happiness
Alyce Pickett

Characters
TODD, ETHAN, KYLA, ages six to eight
SHERI, five years old
KATHY, eleven or twelve years old
MRS. LEAMON, mother

Time: A few days before Christmas

Scene: Den at Kathy Leamon's home

Scene 1

SHERI: I'm so glad it's Christmastime. I love Christmas!
TODD: Yeah, me too. The toy stores have the greatest toys at the mall this year. The ones I like cost a lot of money, though.
KYLA: I picked out what I want and made a list. When Mom saw it she said, "No way you'll get all of that."
ETHAN: I'm just asking for four things this year.
KATHY *(laughing):* You sound like I did when I was a little kid. I spent all of the month before Christmas thinking about what I wanted for Christmas, and being sure my folks knew exactly what I wanted.
SHERI: Don't you still want things for Christmas? You're not all that grown-up.
ETHAN: It wouldn't be Christmas if you didn't get gifts.
KYLA: Some people don't have money to buy gifts . . . or even food. So they don't have Christmas.
KATHY: Oh, yes they do. Jesus was the first Christmas Gift . . . for everyone, but it didn't end then. Every Christmas we remember we still have God's Gift and His love . . . every year. He's the greatest Christmas gift for all time.
TODD: I guess that's the reason people seem happier at Christmas. Even Mr. Tanner seemed happy today. He always frowns and yells at kids when they're noisy, but when we passed his house today he waved at us and even smiled.

KATHY: It's the Christmas spirit all right. I know something that will make us happy even if we don't get all the things we want.
ETHAN: What is it?
OTHERS: Tell us.
KATHY: Make someone else happy.
KYLA: How can we do that?
KATHY: I did it last year by wrapping a little gift for an older lady on my street who lives alone. She seemed so happy that I cared about her, it made me happy too. I talked with her a few minutes and she is really a fun person. I still go back to see her sometimes.
ETHAN: I know an older couple who live on our block, but I don't know what they'd like.
TODD: Mr. Tanner is old, but I can't wrap things.
SHERI: I can't wrap things very good, or write people's names, either.
KATHY: I know what we can do. Everybody bring your things here, then Mom and I will help wrap all of them. On Christmas Eve you can take your gift to your new friend.
KYLA: What kind of things can we get?
KATHY: Ask your mothers. They may have something an older person would like or they might bake cookies for them.
ETHAN: When will we wrap them?
KATHY: Come back Friday and bring what you want wrapped. All right?
OTHERS: Yeah.

(All leave calling "good-by" as they go.)

Scene 2

Kathy and Sheri at table with paper, tape, ribbons, scissors, etc.

SHERI: I'm giving Mrs. McNeil this scarf. *(Holds it up.)* Do you think she'll like it?
KATHY: It's beautiful. She'll love it.
TODD *(enters bringing box and paper):* Mom and I have these for Mr. Tanner. *(Opens box.)*
SHERI: Oh, they look yummy.
KATHY: They smell great too.
TODD: They're my favorite cookies.
KATHY: He'll like them. I bet he doesn't try baking cookies. *(Laughs.)* Maybe he'll be smiling more often.
TODD: I bet he'll be surprised.

(Ethan and Kyla enter bringing packages.)

ETHAN: Mom says Mr. Powers likes to do puzzles, so she got this puzzle book for him and a box of stationery for Mrs. Powers. I put the mints in.

KATHY: They'll like that.

KYLA: I brought a box of greeting cards and some stamps so Mrs. Hale can mail them.

KATHY: That's a thoughtful gift for someone who can't go shopping.

SHERI: Let's wrap everything. *(Jumps up.)*

KATHY: Right. *(Calls out.)* Mom, we're ready.

MRS. LEAMON *(enters and greets the children)*: At your service. Who will be first?

KATHY: Sheri came first and she's the youngest.

MRS. LEAMON: All right. We'll begin with Sheri. Let's get to work. *(Reaches for Sheri's gift and starts wrapping it as others watch.)* Say, why don't we sing a Christmas carol as we wrap. Which song does everybody know?

(Children select a carol and all begin to sing.)

Curtain.

The Truth About Christmas
Carolyn R. Scheidies

Characters: Chorus can be made up of all elementary children or older children with no other parts; Narrator, Mary, Joseph, Juniors 2 (5th & 6th), Preschoolers, Primaries, Juniors 1 (3rd & 4th)

Scene and Time: Contemporary, Now

Props: Bible; biblical costumes for Mary, Joseph, shepherds; manger; staffs; baby doll

Chorus files on stage to risers, if available, singing Christmas carols: "Come Thou Long-Expected Jesus," "It Came upon the Midnight Clear," "Angels, from the Realms of Glory"

(Juniors 2 arrange themselves in three groups/rows: 1—low voices, 2—medium voices, 3—high voices.)

1: Christmas comes but once a year,
3: With bells and lights and holiday cheer.
   And yet somehow each year it seems
2: Fewer and fewer understand what it means.
1: They sing about peace and love and light
1 & 2: Without mentioning the Baby who was born that night.
2: A red-nosed deer and stockings decorate the marquee,
3: While the nativity scene is hidden . . .
1: Behind the tree.
2: And lost, out of view, is the Christmas truth,
3: Christmas is . . . really . . . all about the Christ who came to earth
1: To save a world in need of a hand
3: Came in the fullness
2 & 3: Of God's own plan.

SONG: "Go, Tell It on the Mountain" *(Juniors either step back into the chorus or file offstage while singing chorus of song three times.)*

NARRATOR: Luke 2:1-5

(Preschoolers file on stage. Each carries a picture of baby Jesus. Optional: Have children color these pictures themselves and present them to their parents after holding them up for the audience to see.)

PRESCHOOLERS: We may be small
   And not so tall,
   But we can sing about baby Jesus,
   Born in a cattle stall.

SONG: "Away in a Manger" *(After song, Preschoolers file offstage to sit with parents.)*

NARRATOR: Isaiah 9:2, 6; Luke 2:6, 7

CHORUS: "Joy to the World" *(Stanzas 1, 4)*

(Mary and Joseph walk slowly up the aisle to front center stage, kneel before a manger. Juniors 1 either file on stage or step forward from chorus and form a semicircle behind manger scene facing the audience. Each Junior says a line, or says them in groups of two or more Juniors.)

JUNIORS 1: In the fields that holy night,
   Shepherds watched their sheep.
   When suddenly the dark cold sky *(Look up.)*
   Burst with heavenly light. *(Raise arms wide with wonder.)*

NARRATOR: Luke 2:8-12

JUNIORS 1: To the shepherds poor, smelly and cold,
   Angels spoke an awesome truth,
   God had come to all humankind,
   Not just those of royal birth.

   They listened to the message,
   Mouths gaping wide,
   And as the angels left them,
   Hurried to the Baby's side.

(Shepherds hurry up the aisle and kneel in front of manger.)

   This was the hope of Israel,
   The hope of all, you see,

The Savior born in Bethlehem
Was born to set us free.

SONG: "Go, Tell It on the Mountain" *(Chorus: sing the chorus; Juniors 1: Stanzas 1 and 2; All: Stanza three and chorus.)*

(Juniors 1 either step back into chorus or file offstage. Primaries step out or file on stage forming two groups, one on either side of the stage angled to face both manger and audience.)

NARRATOR: Luke 2:15-17

GROUP 1: The shepherds rejoiced at the sight of the Child,
GROUP 2: But did they fully comprehend,
    The Baby born in Bethlehem,
GROUP 1: Came not as conquering hero,
BOTH: But as Savior, Lord and Friend.
    "I have come that they may have life, and have it to the full"
    (John 10:10 NIV).

SONG: "O Thou Joyful, O Thou Wonderful" *(Primaries: Stanza 1; Chorus: Stanza 2 and All: Stanza 3)*

SONG: "Hark! the Herald Angels Sing" *(Optional)*

NARRATOR: Luke 2:14

(Juniors 2 arrange themselves in three groups: 1—low voices; 2—medium voices, 3—high voices.)

1: That's the truth about Christmas.
3: It's not about gifts and Christmas lights,
2: But about the very Light of the world
1 & 2: And the gift of eternal life.
2: For the infant born in Bethlehem was
3: Not just any baby born in a stall,
1: But Jesus, the Savior who died and rose again,
ALL: To save us one and all.
ALL *(including chorus)*: John 3:16.

SONG: "Go, Tell It on the Mountain" *(Chorus only. Ask audience to join in.)*

Thanksgiving

A Little Rhyme
Dolores Steger

Here is just a little rhyme:
Hooray! It is Thanksgiving time.

The Great Things
Dolores Steger

Praise, give thanks now
    everyone,
For all the great things God has
    done.

Day of Thanks
Helen C. Shambaugh

On this day of thanks,
My hands can fold in prayer,
    (Fold hands.)
While I bow my head and say,
    (Bow head.)
Thank You God, for Your care.

For All the Things
Dolores Steger

Thanksgiving is a special day,
    It gives us all a chance to say,
Thank You, Lord, for all the
    things
  That Your kindness to us
    brings.

The Splendor of Thanksgiving
Dolores Steger

The splendor of Thanksgiving
  Is very clear to me;
It is my chance to thank the Lord
  For all He's given me.

A Prayer
Dolores Steger

My Thanksgiving prayer for you
  Is so simple, I'll just say,
May you be very thankful for
  God's blessings sent your way.

What Am I Most Thankful For?
Dolores Steger

What am I most thankful for?
  I'll tell you earnestly,
I am most thankful for the Lord
  Who loves and cares for me.

Blessings
Dolores Steger

God's wonderful blessings I am
    thankful for;
I wonder how many more He
    has in store?

Your Feast
Dolores Steger

When enjoying your feast,
  I'm hoping you may
Thank God for providing it
  Thanksgiving Day.

Things to Be Thankful For
Orpha A. Thomas

Be thankful for the rain that falls
  that makes the flowers grow.
Be thankful for the sunshine and
  for the sparkling snow.
For home and food and family
  and for the birds that sing.
There's so much to be thankful
  for, I can't think of everything.

Have a Thankful Heart
Cora M. Owen

Sing to the Lord and bless His
  name
All of His good news to proclaim.
Pour out your thanks from day
  to day,
For all you have to bless your
  way.

Sing to the Lord your songs of
  praise.
He gives to us in many ways.
A thankful heart will always
  please.
So let your heart be one of these.

Before We Eat Our Turkey
Dolores Steger

Before we eat our turkey
  On Thanksgiving Day,
We fold our hands and bow our
  heads,
  And to the Lord we pray.
We thank Him for the blessings
  He showers from above,
But most of all we thank Him
  For His deep, abiding love.

Happy Thanksgiving
Kay Hoffman

The pumpkin pies are cooling
  Upon the pantry shelf
While Mother scurries to and fro
  Much like a busy elf.

We've casseroles of golden yams
  And scalloped corn to bake,
Cranberry sauce, plum pudding
  And stuffing yet to make.

Tomorrow when the kinfolk
  come,
  The rafters surely will ring.
We'll offer thanks, and then
  we'll eat
  Till we can hardly sing.

Mid fellowship and hearty meal
  And snowflakes on the way,
May every home be warmly
  blessed
  On this Thanksgiving Day.

Protect Me
Lillian Robbins

Thank You, Lord, for the food
   we eat
  And the houses where we live,
For the friends we have and the
   fun we share,
  All the blessings You kindly
   give.

Help me to be a child to please
  And walk in the way that's
   right.
And when I lay me down to
   sleep,
  Protect me through the night.
   Amen.

Make Thanksgiving More
Helen C. Shambaugh

Thanksgiving should be more,
Than turkey, pies and such,
Football games, parades, and
   autumns golden touch.
For we should always remember,
From God all good things come,
Thank Him for blessing our
   nation, families and home.
Greater yet, we have a Savior,
Who is God's only Son!
With grateful hearts, we thank
   You, Lord,
For allowing Jesus to come.

Prepare the Feast
Dolores Steger

Prepare the feast; the day has
   come
  To celebrate and praise,
With thankful hearts, the
   blessings
  That the Lord to us displays.

Prepare the feast; delight in it,
  Remembering as you do,
The Lord feeds all and He
   prepares
  A feast in Heaven, too.

Approaching Thanksgiving Time
Nell Ford Hann

Leaves have changed their colors
  Now the trees are bare again;
Approaching Thanksgiving time,
  The evening chill sets in.

The crops are gathered from the
   fields,
Pumpkins—orange, apples—
   red-gold;
Geese heading south . . . corn
   fodder shocks,
  Enrichments I behold.

Visions of apple-bobbing,
  Pumpkin pies come to mind;
As we give God thanks for the
   bumper crop,
  Approaching Thanksgiving
   time.

Talk to Jesus
Helen C. Shambaugh

I'm going to bow my head,
   And fold my hands to pray,
'Cause I want to talk to Jesus
   On this special day. *(Bows head
   and folds hands.)*

Thank You Jesus, for Your love.
   When You hear Your people
      pray,
May the sound of their thanks
      giving,
   Give You a happy
      Thanksgiving Day! Amen.

I Can Say Thank You
Carolyn R. Scheidies

I can thank Him for my food,
Thank Him for all I see,
Oh, yes, I thank You, Jesus,
For all my family.

But I don't just want to thank
   Him
On Thanksgiving Day,
I'm going to thank my Jesus
Each day of the year.
Thank You, Jesus!

Thankful People
Cora M. Owen

Thankful people don't forget
   To thank the Lord each day.
For all blessings that He sends,
   To brighten all their way.

Thankful people always tell,
   What God has done for them.
And praise God for all things
   Which from His goodness
      stem.

Thanks Each and Every Day
Dolores Steger

I've stuffed myself with turkey,
With corn bread, pumpkin pie,
And now I'm, oh, so very full
That much I can't deny;
I'm full of thankfulness it's true,
And so to God I say,
Thanks on this Thanksgiving
And thanks each and every day.

God Is Great and Good
Cora M. Owen

"God is great and God is good,"
So little children pray.
Let us be just like a child,
And say the same today.

"God is great and God is good."
Let's thank Him from the heart,
Just the way the children do.
Now is the time to start.

Don't Ever Forget
Cora M. Owen

Oh, give thanks unto the Lord,
  For He is good.
Remember to say, "thank you"
  As we all should.

Praise Him for your benefits,
  Which will not cease.
Thank Him as He blesses you,
  With joy and peace.

Thank Him for the things He
    gives
  For every day.
Remember how He provides,
  For all your way.

Count Your Blessings
Nell Ford Hann

Count your blessings,
  Day by day;
For friends and family,
  Near and far away.
For love and joy,
  For children's giggles;
For precious little puppies,
  With tiny tails that wiggles.
For pats on the back,
  For helping hands;
For things that occur,
  Only God understands.
Count your blessings,
  Count them joys untold;
Blessings, my child,
  Much purer than gold.

Gather the Harvest
Dolores Steger

Gather the harvest into the barn;
  It's autumn, a chill's in the air;
Gather the harvest into the barn,
  So safely it will be stored there.

Then gather the harvest into the
    home;
  The time for preparing is here,
Then gather the harvest into the
    home;
  The time for a feast's drawing
    near.

Now gather the harvest into the
    heart,
  Where there it will evermore
    stay,
Now gather the harvest into the
    heart;
  Thanking God for each
    Thanksgiving Day.

Without Thanksgiving Day
Dolores Steger

How very sad the world would
    be
  Without Thanksgiving Day,
Without turkey, pumpkin pie,
  Without a time to say
"Thank You for Your wonders,
    Lord,
  Your tender, loving care.
Thank You for the blessings,
    Lord,
  You shower everywhere."

Thanksgiving Every Day
Pauline Pickering

Harvesttime and Thanksgiving
  will soon be here.
But Christians are thankful all
  through the year.
Giving thanks for our daily
  bread,
And thanks for a place to lay
  our heads.
Giving thanks for friends, neigh-
  bors and loved ones,
And thanks for God's only Son;
Whom He sent to earth to
  redeem us
From our sins, His name is
  Jesus.
We especially thank Him each
  Lord's day,
As we commune with Him and
  pray
For His coming again, maybe
  soon
Maybe in the morning or night
  or noon.
What a happy day that will be,
When His glorious face we see.
Until then, be it early, midday or
  late;
We'll continue to pray and
  celebrate.

I Don't Like Turkey
Lillian Robbins

Ugh! I don't like turkey
  And cranberry sauce.
And all those greens?
  I hope they get lost.

Just bring on the pizza
  And ice cream galore.
Maybe a cookie or two;
  I could eat some more.

You may agree with me,
  But it is quite true,
If I don't eat veggies,
  Mom's in a stew.

Yes, I am thankful
  On this special day.
To God up above
  I'm willing to pray.

Anyway, God,
  Just send me what's good.
I'll try to live right
  And do what I should.

To all of you here,
  I share this wish.
Thank God for His blessings
  And dig your favorite dish.

That's cool! Happy
  Thanksgiving.

Thankful for Jesus
Helen C. Shambaugh

(This may be a recitation for one child or for five children holding a picture relating to each verse.)

When I fold my hands
  And bow my head to pray,
Mommy says Jesus hears me,
  Yes, every word I say.

When I'm lying in my bed,
  Alone in the dark of night,
Daddy says Jesus is with me,
  And will always be my light.

When I visit Grandma,
  She holds me in her arms,
She tells me Jesus loves me;
  He will keep me from all harm.

When I help Granddad feed the birds,
  He always says to me,
"Be kind to all God's creatures.
  Jesus made them for you and me."

So I'm thankful for my parents,
  For my grandparents too,
But I'm most thankful for Jesus;
  He's with me whatever I do!

Thanksgiving Day Is Cool
Helen C. Shambaugh

Thanksgiving Day is lots of fun,
  First off, I'm out of school!
And all the good stuff that we eat
  Wow!! That's really cool!

Aww—I know there's more to it,
  Sure, it's a patriotic holiday.
When the Pilgrims came to this country
  They set aside this special day.

So thankful that God had blessed them,
  With this country as their home,
They planned a feast to celebrate God,
  For all the good He had done.

It's a day for people to gather,
  In remembrance of God above,
To join together in humble thanks,
  For all of His great love.

Now that I really think of it,
  I see Thanksgiving in a new way,
That makes it even more cool to me,
  Have a happy Thanksgiving Day!

Thanks to Jesus
Alyce Pickett

CHILD 1:
I'm so glad You came to be
Friend and Lord on earth for me.

CHILD 2:
I'm thankful, too, because I know
You're with me everywhere I go.

CHILD 3:
Thank You for listening when I pray
And for the love You give each day.

The Meaning of Thanksgiving
Carolyn R. Scheidies

ALL: The meaning of Thanksgiving is so very clear,

CHILD 1 *(Holds up picture of family around table):*
A day overflowing with food and family.

CHILD 2 *(Holds up picture of hands folded in prayer):*
And heart overflowing with thanks.

CHILD 3 *(Holds up picture of Jesus):*
To Jesus who gave us all these.

SONG: "Count Your Blessings"
(All sing first and last stanzas.)

Bless Our Church
Helen Kitchell Evans

FIRST CHILD:
God bless our church.

SECOND CHILD:
Our fine leaders, too.

BOTH:
They serve the church with devotion so true.

FIRST CHILD:
God bless our church.

SECOND CHILD:
Please help us grow,

BOTH:
It takes everyone working. That we all know.

FIRST CHILD:
God bless our church!

SECOND CHILD:
May God bless it each day.

BOTH:
For the growth of our church
Let us all pray.

(Follow with a prayer and the song "The Church's One Foundation" or a song of the director's choice. Congregation may join in if so desired.)

The Bible Speaks of Thankfulness
Dorothy M. Page

Characters:
READER: Person with good speaking voice and with the ability to read well. (Can be dressed in Bible-times robe.)
NINE CHILDREN: Each carries a placard with lettering large enough for the audience to read. The words are shown below.

Scriptures are from the *King James Version* of the Bible.

The Scriptures and placards list good things from God we are thankful for.

READER *(wearing robe, reading from scroll):* "And Jesus took the loaves; and when he had given thanks, he distributed to the disciples, and the disciples to them that were set down; and likewise of the fishes as much as they would" (John 6:11).

(Child 1 marches in and goes to extreme right or left side of stage holding his placard which reads THANKS FOR FOOD in front.)

READER: "I thank my God upon every remembrance of you" (Philippians 1:3).

(Child 2 marches in and stands next to Child 1. Placard reads AUTOMATIC THANKS. As each Child enters he moves to stand next to the preceding Child.)

READER: "Then they took away the stone . . . Jesus lifted up his eyes, and said, Father, I thank thee that thou hast heard me" (John 11:41).

(Child 3 marches in carrying placard reading ANSWERED PRAYER.)

READER: "Giving thanks always for all things unto God and the Father in the name of our Lord Jesus Christ" (Ephesians 5:20).

(Child 4 enters carrying placard reading IN CHRIST'S NAME.)

READER: "In every thing give thanks: for this is the will of God in Christ Jesus concerning you" (1 Thessalonians 5:18).

(Child 5 enters with placard reading GOD'S WILL.)

READER: "O give thanks unto the LORD; for he is good: because his mercy endureth for ever" (Psalm 118:1).

(Child 6 enters with placard reading MERCY.)

READER: "I thank thee, and praise thee, O thou God of my fathers, who hast given me wisdom and might" (Daniel 2:23).

(Child 7 enters with placard reading WISDOM.)

READER: "Enter into his gates with thanksgiving, and into his courts with praise: be thankful unto him, and bless his name. For the LORD is good; his mercy is everlasting; and his truth endureth to all generations" (Psalm 100:4, 5).

(Child 8 enters with placard reading TRUTH.)

READER: "We are bound to thank God always for you, brethren, as it is meet, because that your faith groweth exceedingly, and the charity of every one of you all toward each other aboundeth" (2 Thessalonians 1:3).

(Child 9 enters with placard reading FAITH and CHARITY. At this point Reader and Children bow heads, fold hands in prayer and repeat in unison:)

ALL: The list of good things you have sent
Is endless, it is true,
Our prayer is our thanksgiving
For blessings, God, from You. Amen.